SUPER
SCIENCE
EXPERIMENTS

Super Science Experiments

Written by Q.L. Pearce

Illustrated by Tony Gleeson

ROXBURY PARK

LOWELL HOUSE JUVENILE

LOS ANGELES

NTC/Contemporary Publishing Group

Published by Lowell House
A division of NTC/Contemporary Publishing Group, Inc.
4255 West Touhy Avenue, Lincolnwood (Chicago), Illinois 60646-1975 U.S.A.

Lowell House books can be purchased at special discounts when ordered in bulk for premiums and special sales. Contact Department CS at the following address:

NTC/Contemporary Publishing Group
4255 West Touhy Avenue
Lincolnwood, IL 60646-1975
1-800-323-4900

ISBN: 0-7373-0073-6
Library of Congress Catalog Card Number: 98-75646

Roxbury Park is a division of NTC/Contemporary Publishing Group, Inc.

Managing Director and Publisher: Jack Artenstein
Editor in Chief, Roxbury Park Books: Michael Artenstein
Director of Publishing Services: Rena Copperman
Editorial Assistant: Nicole Monastirsky
Interior Designer: Brenda Leach

Printed and bound in the United States of America
10 9 8 7 6 5 4 3 2

Contents

INTRODUCTION

Note to Parents

Super Science Experiments is the perfect supplement to the classroom science curriculum. It is filled with hands-on experiments that will spark your child's interest and curiosity in his or her environment. Each activity has been designed to be safe and simple, requiring materials that are inexpensive and readily available. If possible, provide an area where often-used items may be stored. Some experiments may be a little messy. Those that involve heat or sharp instruments, perhaps requiring adult supervision or participation, are marked by asterisks.

At the beginning of the book, there is a list of materials needed for many of the experiments, followed by a section on safety sense. It is a good idea to review these segments with your child before he or she begins the first activity.

After an experiment has been completed, ask questions about how and why it worked as it did. Encouraging youngsters to formulate their own ideas will promote understanding of the basic concepts illustrated by each activity.

About This Book

Why do things work the way they do? Things happen for reasons that may not be clear at first. Men and women are working in every branch of science to discover the answers. The best way to find out is through observation and experimentation. First you must have a question: then you think of a way to find the answer. Each of the experiments that follow start with a question. Read the activity through completely before you begin, and be sure you have all the materials at hand. Sometimes finding an answer will lead to more questions. If so, go ahead and design your own experiments and keep a notebook to record your results. Have fun!

Your Science Lab

The kitchen is the best place to perform most experiments. Certain things you will need, such as running water, are available. In some cases you may need to heat things on the stove or cool them in the refrigerator. Many of your supplies are probably in the home already. Ask an adult before you use household materials.

Here is a list of some of the items you may need for your physics laboratory:

✓ chopping board for cutting

✓ salt, food coloring, baking soda, vinegar, sugar, liquid detergent

✓ saucepan, pie plate, clean glass jam or jelly jars with lids, measuring cups, measuring spoons, wooden spoon, drinking glass, mixing bowls

✓ string, tape, paper clips, balloons, small glass tank, rubber bands, plastic straws, scissors, eyedropper, sieve, thermometer, magnifying glass, stopwatch or clock with a second hand, scale, compass, clothespins, wire cutters, rubber tubing, knife, tweezers

✓ pot holder, gloves, apron, newspaper, notebook, pencils, marking pen, hot pad, drawing compass

✓ Plaster of Paris, potting soil, lima beans, and limewater

The last two items can be purchased at a pharmacy. It is a good idea to have several growing plants ready for use. Geraniums are an excellent sample potted plant. Elodea, a water plant available at pet stores that sell tropical fish, is also useful.

For certain experiments, you may need some materials that are not mentioned here. Read through the list at the beginning of each activity before you begin.

Safety Sense

Here are a few simple rules you should always follow in your laboratory:

✓ Read the experiment through completely before you begin.

✓ Wear old clothing or an apron.

✓ Cover your work area with newspaper.

✓ Never put an unknown material in your mouth or near your eyes.

✓ Clean your work area and instruments when you are finished.

✓ Wash your hands after each experiment.

✓ If an experiment will need a long time to finish, find a place where it will not be in the way of other family members.

✓ For some experiments, you may need help. These are marked with an asterisk (*).

Learning About Energy

One of the most basic of the sciences is physics. This is the study of the relationship between the matter and energy that make up our universe and the forces that affect them. Most other branches of science, including chemistry, geology, and astronomy, depend on the laws of physics.

Did You Know?

Here are a few of those laws that have been discovered and how they have been applied.

Light always travels at the same speed. Light travels through space at about 186,000 miles per second. If you know how long a beam of light takes to reach a certain point, you can figure out how far away that point is. During the Apollo Moon missions, special mirrors were positioned on the surface of the moon. Astronomers on earth were able to shoot a laser beam, bounce it off the moon mirrors and back to earth. By recording the amount of time it took for the beam to travel from the earth to the moon and back, they could figure out the exact distance between our planet and its satellite.

A body in motion will stay in motion unless it is acted on by a force. This law means that once something is moving, it will continue to move in the same direction and at the same speed unless something else stops it or changes its motion. Knowing this law helped scientists to plan the Voyager Space Probe's course to the outer planets. They knew that Voyager would keep moving outward but its course could be changed by the effect of the gravitational pull of planets as it flew by them.

A current of moving electrons produces a magnetic field. This knowledge led to the development of electromagnets (you'll get to make one of these later in the book). Electromagnets are used to do work in many ways, such as in the ignition systems in cars, in telephones and televisions, and in radar equipment.

There are natural magnets, too. Let's start our experiments by finding out about magnets and magnetism.

Learning About Earth

Scientist who study nature are concerned with the materials that make up Earth, the events that shape it, and the plants and animals that live on it. Our Earth is unlike any other planet in the Solar System because it is the only one known to support life. Living things inhabit the air, land, and sea. Any place on the planet where life is found, from the deepest waters of the ocean to the highest mountain tops, is part of Earth's BIO-SPHERE.

The first living things to appear on Earth were probably microscopic single-celled organisms much like bacteria. These eventually developed into an algaelike form now known as blue-greens. These blue-greens contained a substance called chlorophyll. With this they were able to absorb light from the Sun and convert it to energy. The energy was used to convert carbon dioxide gas and water to food. This process is called PHOTOSYNTHESIS.

Except for fungi, modern plants use photosynthesis to produce food, too. Let's start our experiments by finding out more about plants.

PART 1

AMAZING ENERGY EXPERIMENTS

MAGNETS AND MAGNETISM

MAGNETIC POWERS
What do magnets attract?

Materials:

✓ magnet
✓ variety of objects, including paper, paper clips, pencil, coins, scissors, plastic cup, bobby pins, steel straight pins, needle, drinking glass, cardboard

Procedure:

1. Look at your objects. Separate them into two groups, one with things you think will be attracted by the magnet, and one with things you think won't be attracted.

2. Touch your magnet to each object. If your guess was correct, leave the object in that group. If you were wrong, place the object in the other group.

3. Look at the group of things that magnets attract. What is something that is alike about all of these items?

WHAT'S HAPPENING HERE

Magnets mainly attract metal objects containing iron, nickel, or cobalt.

HARD WORK
Can some things block out magnetism?

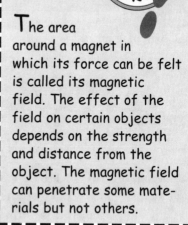

Materials:

- ✓ magnet
- ✓ paper clip
- ✓ aluminum
- ✓ paper
- ✓ saucepan
- ✓ plastic cup
- ✓ wooden ruler
- ✓ handkerchief
- ✓ stainless steel
- ✓ cookie sheet
- ✓ drinking glass

The area around a magnet in which its force can be felt is called its magnetic field. The effect of the field on certain objects depends on the strength and distance from the object. The magnetic field can penetrate some materials but not others.

Procedure:

1. Try to pick up each of the materials with the magnet. Do any of them "stick"?

2. Place a paper clip under a piece of paper. Using your magnet, touch the paper directly over the clip. Try lifting the paper at this spot. What happens?

3. Try the same thing using the handkerchief over the clip.

4. Place the paper clip in the plastic cup. Touch the magnet to the cup directly under the clip. What happens? Can you move the clip around with your magnet?

5. Try the same thing using the glass. Try it with water in the glass, too. What happens?

6. Put the clip on the ruler. Put your magnet below it. Can your magnet move the clip through the wood? Now try the cookie sheet and the saucepan. Is there a difference?

MAGNETIC POLES
Which parts of the magnet work best?

Materials:

✓ bar magnet
✓ a variety of metal objects such as pins, paper clips, steel wool (without soap)

Procedure:

1. Spread the objects out on a table.

2. Hold the magnet lengthwise. Move the magnet slightly above one of the objects, then lift the magnet. Repeat this with each of the objects.

3. To which part of the magnet do most of the objects stick?

4. Which part of the magnet was strong enough to lift each of the materials? Are the ends (called poles) or the middle of the magnet stronger?

The force of a magnet is concentrated at its ends, or poles.

NORTH AND SOUTH
Are both magnetic poles the same?

Materials:

✓ compass   ✓ 2 bar magnets   ✓ string   ✓ crayon

Procedure:

1. Use the compass to find out which direction is due north.

2. Tie a piece of string around the center of your magnet so that it hangs level. Hold the loose end or tie it to something so that the magnet can spin freely. Which end or pole is pointing north when it stops turning? With the crayon, mark that end *N* for north, and the other end *S* for south. (This is important to remember for further experiments.)

3. Spin the magnet again. Does the end marked *N* still point north? Do the same experiment with the other magnet and mark each end with *N* or *S*.

4. Hold the magnets so that both north poles are pointed toward each other. Do like poles attract each other or push each other away?

5. Point both south poles toward each other. What happens?

6. Remove the markings from one of the magnets. Now bring the two magnets close together. Are they attracted to each other or repelled? Can you guess which pole is which on the unmarked magnet by how it reacts to the marked one?

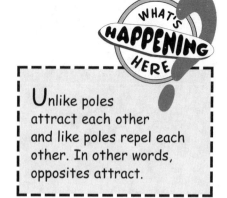

WHAT'S HAPPENING HERE?

Unlike poles attract each other and like poles repel each other. In other words, opposites attract.

MAGNETIC FIELD
What is a magnetic field shaped like?

Materials:
- ✓ steel wool pads
- ✓ old scissors
- ✓ 2 bar magnets with the poles labeled
- ✓ a sheet of plain paper

Procedure:

1. Cut the steel wool into tiny bits with the scissors. Place the magnet on a table and hold the sheet of paper slightly above it. Sprinkle the steel wool bits on the paper. Does a pattern form?

2. Move the paper away from the magnet and gently shake it. Does the pattern disappear? Place the paper above the magnet again. What happens?

3. Move the paper away again, place the second magnet near the first with the north and south poles facing each other, and hold the paper over both magnets. Is the pattern of the steel wool bits different this time?

4. Turn one magnet so that both north poles are facing each other. Does the pattern change?

WHAT'S HAPPENING HERE?

The steel wool clippings are attracted to the lines of force, or magnetic field, around the magnet. The pattern you see is the shape of the magnetic field.

FUN WITH MAGNETS
Do you know how to make a magnet move?

Magnets can be used to make work easier by pushing and pulling heavy loads. Sometimes magnets can keep things in place, and magnets are used in some modern trains to move cars of people safely from place to place.

Here are some things you can make that use magnets.

MAGNETIC PUPPET SHOW

Materials:

- ✓ lightweight cardboard
- ✓ scissors
- ✓ tape
- ✓ 2 bar magnets
- ✓ shoe box
- ✓ paperclips
- ✓ crayons and marking pens

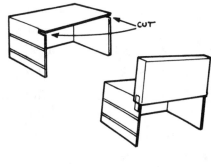

Procedure:

1. Prepare your stage by cutting out one side of the shoe box. Turn the box upside down and make one inch cuts along each back edge as illustrated. Draw a scene on the inside of the lid and color it. Now slip the lid into the cuts you made and tape it securely.

2. Draw two characters on the cardboard and color each. Cut them out, leaving a tab of cardboard at the bottom. Fold the tab so that each figure can stand up, and slip a paper clip over each tab.

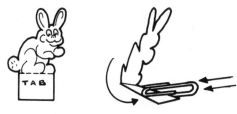

3. Place your characters on the stage. By moving the bar magnets in the shoe box, you can make the figures move and act out a story.

MAGNET RACERS

Materials:

- ✓ cardboard box
- ✓ large paper clip
- ✓ bar magnet
- ✓ glue
- ✓ cardboard
- ✓ pebbles and bits of wood
- ✓ scissors
- ✓ marking pen
- ✓ stopwatch

Procedure:

1. Turn the box upside down and cut away one side so that you can reach into it. On the top, draw a twisting race track about one inch wide. Mark one end START and the other end FINISH. Glue down pebbles and bits of wood as barriers and traps along the route to make it more difficult.

2. Fold a piece of cardboard and draw a race car on one side with the top along the fold. Color and cut out the car.

3. Pull up the center of the paper clip and twist it until it looks like the one in the illustration. Slide your car over the clip and glue it together.

4. Place the car at the beginning of the track. Use the magnet under the box to move the car along. Start the stopwatch and see how long it takes you to complete the track. Take turns racing with your friends to see who can make the best time.

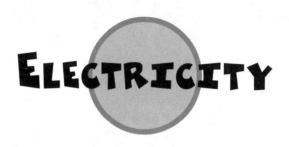

ELECTRICITY

CHARGE IT
Do electrically charged objects attract nonmetal objects?

Materials:

✓ plastic comb   ✓ small bits of paper   ✓ wool fabric

Procedure:

1. Hold the comb over the small pieces of paper for a moment. Does anything happen? Turn on the kitchen tap slowly so that there is a steady stream of water. Hold the comb as close to the stream as you can without getting it wet. Does anything happen now?

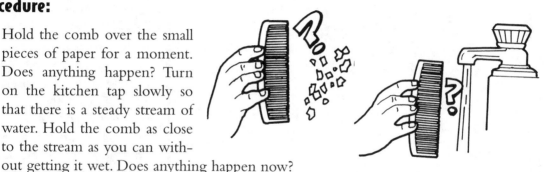

2. Rub the comb briskly with the wool fabric.

3. Hold it over the pieces of paper. They stick to the comb.

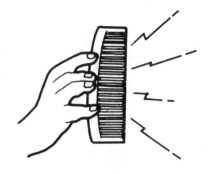

(continued next page)

4. Rub the comb again with the wool and hold it near the stream of water. What happens this time? The comb contains a stored charge of static electricity. It attracts things with a different charge.

5. Lightening is caused by static electricity. To make your own lightening, turn on the kitchen tap after dark. Comb your hair several times, then place the comb near running water. A spark will jump from the comb to the water. You will see the spark more easily if you don't turn on the light. This experiment will work best when the weather is dry.

WHAT'S HAPPENING HERE?

One of the most basic properties of electricity is charge. Charge can be negative or positive. Objects with opposite charge are attracted to each other and those with like charge repel. Electrons have a negative charge. They are tiny particles that orbit the center of atoms. Protons (tiny particles in the center of atoms) have a positive charge. An atom with fewer electrons than protons is positively charged. An atom with more electrons than protons is negatively charged. Atoms with an even number of both are neutral. Static electricity is the buildup of either negative or positive charge in a substance.

LIKE MAGIC
Can static electricity do work?

Materials:

- ✓ 5 x 5 inch square of paper
- ✓ 1 sharp pencil
- ✓ piece of wool fabric
- ✓ modeling clay
- ✓ thread
- ✓ comb
- ✓ 2 balloons
- ✓ scissors

Procedure:

1. Fold the paper and cut it as shown in the drawing to form a star. Push the eraser end of the pencil into the ball of clay so that it will stand. Balance the paper star on the point of the pencil.

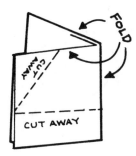

2. Run the comb through your hair several times or rub it with the fabric. Hold the comb near but not touching the star and make a circle around it. The star will begin to move. Do you know what is causing it to spin?

3. Hold a piece of thread in one hand. With the other hand, comb your hair quickly, then pass the comb over the thread. It will rise up and follow the comb. The thread is attracted to the comb.

(continued next page)

4. Blow up both balloons and tie one to each end of a long piece of thread. Holding the thread in the center, allow the balloons to dangle. Do they touch? Quickly rub each balloon on your hair. Dangle the balloons again. Will they touch each other now?

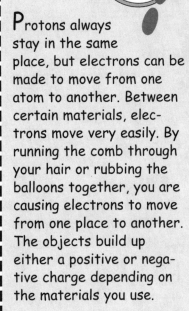

W HAT'S HAPPENING HERE?

Protons always stay in the same place, but electrons can be made to move from one atom to another. Between certain materials, electrons move very easily. By running the comb through your hair or rubbing the balloons together, you are causing electrons to move from one place to another. The objects build up either a positive or negative charge depending on the materials you use.

LIGHT

BENDING LIGHT
Does light always move in a straight line?

Materials:
- ✓ square glass container or tank
- ✓ large piece of white cardboard or paper
- ✓ pencil   ✓ flashlight   ✓ milk

Procedure:

1. Fill the tank with water. Hold the pencil half in and half out of the water. Does it appear to bend?

2. Look at the pencil from different angles. Does the pencil seem to change depending on how you look at it? Look at it from directly above. Does the part in the water appear closer than it should be?

3. Remove the pencil. Hold the white paper about an inch from one side of the tank. On the opposite side, hold the flashlight straight and shine it directly through the water at the paper. The beam will not appear to bend.

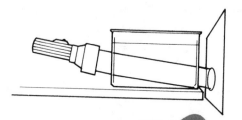

4. Tilt the flashlight slightly upward. Does the beam bend? Which way does it bend? Add a little milk to the water and the light beam will be seen more clearly.

WHAT'S HAPPENING HERE

As light rays travel from air to water or water to air at certain angles, they are slowed and bent slightly. This is called refraction.

ENERGY YOU CAN SEE
What color is light?

Materials:

- ✓ tall glass
- ✓ 3 x 5 inch index card
- ✓ scissors
- ✓ tape
- ✓ large sheet of white paper

Procedure:

1. A beam of white light is made up of many colors that our brain perceives as one. To break a beam of light into its individual colors, cut a one-inch-wide three-inch-long rectangle from a white 3 x 5 inch index card with the scissors.

2. Tape the card to the glass so that the opening is directly over the rim.

3. Fill the glass with water and set it on the ledge or on a table in front of a sunny window. Place the white paper on the floor in front of the glass. The colors will be reflected individually onto the white card under the glass. How many colors do you see? These colors make up the visible spectrum.

WHAT'S HAPPENING HERE?

Sunlight is made up of many different colors of light. Each of these different colors vibrate at a slightly different speed. When the sunlight passes through the water in the glass, each of the colors is slowed and bent. The colors that vibrate faster are bent more than the colors that vibrate slower. Blue and violet rays bend the most, and red the least.

FUN WITH LIGHT*
Up Periscope

Sometimes light does not pass through an object, but is bounced back. This is called reflection. Mirrors can be used to bounce light rays. Follow these directions to make your own periscope and you will be able to see around corners!

Materials:*
- ✓ quart milk carton   ✓ scissors   ✓ tape
- ✓ 2 square pocket mirrors that fit inside the carton

Procedure:

1. Clean out the milk carton carefully.

2. Cut the carton in half. In each half, cut a small hole near the bottom. Slip in a mirror and tape it faceup at about a forty-five degree angle slanting toward the hole.

3. Tape the carton securely together again so that one hole is at the top of one side and the other hole is at the bottom of the opposite side.

4. Kneel down behind a chair and aim one hole over the back. Look through the other hole. What do you see?

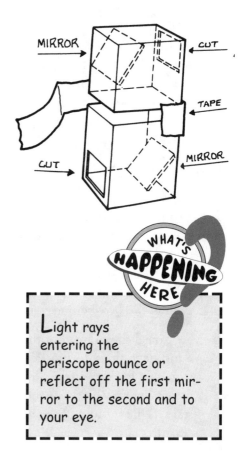

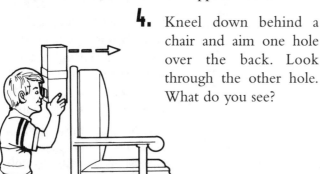

WHAT'S HAPPENING HERE?

Light rays entering the periscope bounce or reflect off the first mirror to the second and to your eye.

19

HEAT

THE HEAT IS ON
What is friction?

Materials:

- ✓ 2 dry sticks of wood, about 8 inches long and 1 inch thick
- ✓ shoe box without lid
- ✓ 3 feet of string
- ✓ scissors
- ✓ brick

Procedure:

1. Hold the two sticks by the ends, one stick in each hand. Cross the sticks over each other and rub back and forth as hard as you can about twenty or thirty times.

2. Stop and feel the area that has been rubbed together. Is it warm?

3. With the scissors, make a small hole in the short side of the shoe box. Tie one end of the string through the hole. Use the string to pull the empty box across a hard surface on the ground such as a sidewalk. Walk slowly back and forth a few times, pulling the box behind you.

4. Stop. Feel the bottom of the box. Is it warm? Wait a moment, then do the experiment again but this time run back and forth quickly. Is there a difference? Put the brick in the box and repeat both steps. Is the bottom of the box warm? Are the sides warm?

WHAT'S HAPPENING HERE

Most surfaces are rough and do not slide easily past each other. If you could look at them through a microscope you would see that even things that seem to be smooth, such as metal or glass, are actually rough. This resistance when you rub surfaces together is called friction. It takes energy to make the surfaces move across each other and much of that energy is turned into heat. Spacecraft returning to Earth through the atmosphere heat up because of friction with the air.

20

KEEPING COOL
Can friction be controlled?

Materials:

- ✓ 2 blocks of wood about 3 inches square
- ✓ soap
- ✓ 2 metal jar lids
- ✓ cooking oil

Procedure:

1. Create friction by rubbing the two blocks of wood together very quickly for a few moments. Feel them. Do they feel warm?

2. Smear soap between the blocks, then rub them together again. Feel them. Did they heat up? Why not? When things slide past each other more easily do they create less heat?

3. Rub the metal lids together. They appear very smooth. Do they heat up? Rub a little oil between the lids, then try again. Did they heat up as much?

WHAT'S HAPPENING HERE

The soap and oil are lubricants. Lubricants are substances used to coat the surfaces between moving objects so that they slide past each other more easily. Lubricants can help prevent machine parts from wearing out.

EXPAND OR CONTRACT*
What happens when a gas becomes hotter?

Materials:*
- ✓ nail   ✓ food coloring   ✓ clay
- ✓ container large enough to hold the bottle
- ✓ bottle with a plastic screw-on cap
- ✓ drinking straw

Procedure:

1. With the nail, make a hole in the bottle cap large enough for the straw to fit through. Fill the bottle halfway with water and add a few drops of food coloring.

2. Screw on the cap, and slide the straw until it is about an inch from the bottom of the bottle. Seal around the cap's edges with clay and plug the hole of the straw too, but make a small hole in the center of the clay with the nail. Do you think you can get the water out of the bottle without tipping it over or taking off the cap?

3. Place the container in the sink because this can be a little messy. Fill the container with very hot water and put the bottle in it. Wait until the air in the bottle warms up. What happens?

WHAT'S HAPPENING HERE

Most things expand or get larger when they heat up. As the warm air in the bottle expanded, it pushed down on the water. This caused some of the water to travel up the straw and spray out of the top of the bottle.

THE BIG STORY*
Do solids expand when heated?

Materials: *

✓ 1 piece of wood about 8 inches long, 6 inches wide, and ¹/₂ inch thick (piece A)

✓ 2 pieces of wood about 4 x 4 inches and ¹/₂ inch thick (pieces B and C)

✓ aluminum rod about 1 foot long   ✓ crayon, pen or pencil

✓ 3 candles   ✓ nails

Procedure:

1. Ask your adult helper to drill a hole in one of the smaller pieces of wood (piece B); then nail the three pieces together as in the illustration, with piece A on the bottom.

2. Fit the aluminum rod into the hole in piece B. Rest the end on a nail driven into piece C. Make a mark on the wood at the end of the rod.

3. Measure the distance between piece A and the rod. Cut the candles one inch shorter than this distance. Place the three candles under the metal rod and light them.

4. After a few minutes, compare the end of the rod with your mark. Is the rod longer? Did the heat from the candles cause it to expand? Make a new mark at the end of the rod and remove the candles.

5. After the metal has cooled completely, check the mark again. What happened?

WHAT'S HAPPENING HERE?

When most materials are heated, the atoms that they are made of move farther apart. This causes the material to expand.

SOUND

DID YOU HEAR THAT?
What is sound?

Materials:
- ✓ balloon
- ✓ rubber band
- ✓ small mirror
- ✓ can opener
- ✓ sugar
- ✓ tape
- ✓ saucepan
- ✓ flashlight
- ✓ metal spoon
- ✓ coffee cans with both ends removed

Procedure:

1. Cut off the bottom of a coffee can. Cut the balloon and stretch it across the top of the opened can. Secure it with a rubber band. Place a teaspoon of sugar in the center. Now holding the saucepan close to the can, bang on it with the spoon. Does the sugar move?

2. Remove the sugar and tape the mirror to the balloon, shiny side up.

3. Set the can on its side on a tabletop. Prop a flashlight in front of it so that the light reflects from the mirror onto the opposite wall.

4. Sing into the back of the can. What happens to the light? Why is it vibrating?

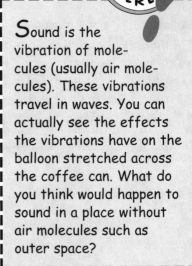

WHAT'S HAPPENING HERE?

Sound is the vibration of molecules (usually air molecules). These vibrations travel in waves. You can actually see the effects the vibrations have on the balloon stretched across the coffee can. What do you think would happen to sound in a place without air molecules such as outer space?

24

HIGH OR LOW
Why are some sounds higher than others?

Materials:
- ✓ ruler
- ✓ rubber band
- ✓ book
- ✓ 2 small erasers

Procedure:

1. Place the ruler on the table with about nine inches beyond the edge and hold it there. Put the book on top of it to hold it in place. Pull down on the end and let it flick up again. Did it make a noise?

2. Push the ruler two inches farther under the book and flick it again. Was the noise higher or lower than the first sound? Push the ruler in two more inches and try it again. As the exposed end gets shorter, what happens to the sound it makes?

3. Pick up the ruler and stretch a rubber band over it lengthwise. Slip an eraser under the band at each end. Pluck at the rubber band. Move the erasers closer together and pluck at the rubber band again. The faster something vibrates, the higher the sound. When you shorten the rubber band is it vibrating faster or slower? How do you know?

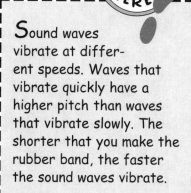

WHAT'S **HAPPENING** HERE

Sound waves vibrate at different speeds. Waves that vibrate quickly have a higher pitch than waves that vibrate slowly. The shorter that you make the rubber band, the faster the sound waves vibrate.

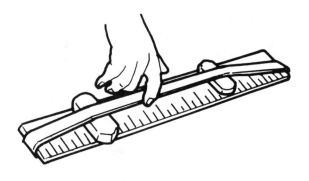

MAKING MUSIC
It's easy to make your own musical instrument.

Materials:

- ✓ ½ gallon milk carton
- ✓ several long, thick and thin rubber bands
- ✓ scissors   ✓ pencil   ✓ tape

Procedure:

1. Cut a hole about three inches wide and four inches long in one side of the milk carton. Tape a pencil across the bottom edge of the hole.

2. Stretch the rubber bands lengthwise around the carton so that part of each one is over the hole, just like in the picture. Put them in order, thick to thin.

3. Each band will have a different sound when you pluck it. You can change its sound by holding the band against the milk carton. This will make the "string" shorter. Will the new sound be higher or lower?

GRAVITY

In science fiction stories, you often hear about "force fields." There are force fields in real life too, such as Earth's magnetic field. Can you think of another force that is very important? It keeps the planets in orbit and holds everything on Earth, even the atmosphere, in place . . . the force is gravity.

HOLD TIGHT
Does gravity pull harder on bigger objects?

Materials:

✓ book ✓ large sponge ✓ tennis ball
✓ rock the size of a tennis ball ✓ scale

Procedure:

1. Hold the book in your outstretched hand. Can you feel gravity pulling down on it? What will happen if you let go of the book?

2. Try lifting the sponge. It is much lighter. Is gravity pulling down on it? Let go of it. What happens?

3. Hold the tennis ball and the rock in your hand. Upon which object does gravity seem to be pulling harder? Does gravity pull harder on objects only because of their size? Is there another difference between the rock and the tennis ball? Weigh each object.

Size alone does not determine how hard gravity pulls on an object. An object's mass is more important. Mass is the amount of particles such as protons, neutrons, and electrons that make up the molecules in a substance. Weight is the measure of the pull of gravity on mass. If two objects are the same size and one is heavier, it is more massive.

FALLING OBJECTS
Do objects of different sizes and weights fall at different speeds?

Materials:

- ✓ scale
- ✓ tennis ball
- ✓ large book
- ✓ block of wood
- ✓ baseball
- ✓ rubber ball
- ✓ large marble
- ✓ sheet of paper
- ✓ ball of crumpled aluminum foil

Procedure:

1. Weigh each of the objects. Are they all different? Stand and hold the tennis ball and the rubber ball at the same level. Drop them to the floor. Do they hit at the same time? Try dropping them from various heights but be sure they always start even.

2. Try the experiments with different combinations of balls. Do they always reach the ground at the same time no matter what size they are?

3. Drop a ball and the square block of wood. Do they hit at the same time? Does it matter that these objects are a different shape?

4. Drop the book and the paper at the same time. It takes longer for the paper to fall because friction with the air is slowing it down.

5. Crumple the paper into a tight ball. Now does it fall at the same rate as the book? What changed about the paper to prevent the air from slowing it down? Does shape have an effect on the rate of fall of certain objects?

WHAT'S HAPPENING HERE

The speed at which objects fall to the ground in a vacuum (an empty space that does not contain any air or any other mass) is the same no matter what the weight of the object. Objects falling through air may be slowed because of their shape. Friction with the air caused the flat piece of paper to fall more slowly. If you crumple the paper into a ball, you lessen this effect.

PERFECTLY BALANCED
What is a center of gravity?

Materials:

✓ potato   ✓ pencil   ✓ 2 forks   ✓ soda bottle

Procedure:

1. Cut a one-inch-thick slice from the center of the potato. Push the pencil through the potato slice about one-half inch from the edge so that it looks like the one in the picture. Try to balance the tip of the pencil off the edge of the table. Will it balance? Is the weight of the potato making it fall?

2. Push a fork into the lower edge of the potato so that it extends underneath the tabletop as in the illustration. Can you make it balance now? You may have to adjust it a few times until you finally get it to balance. Did you change the center of gravity of the object? How?

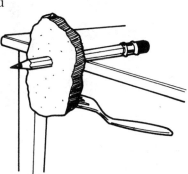

3. Remove the pencil from the potato. Place the bottle in the center of the table. Try to balance the pencil on its tip on top of the bottle. Now push the pencil through the center of the potato slice. Insert two forks into the edge directly opposite each other and try it again. Can you make up some of your own balancing acts?

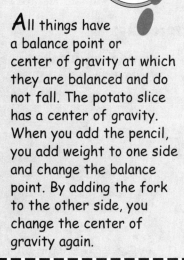

What's HAPPENING HERE?

All things have a balance point or center of gravity at which they are balanced and do not fall. The potato slice has a center of gravity. When you add the pencil, you add weight to one side and change the balance point. By adding the fork to the other side, you change the center of gravity again.

29

AT THE CENTER
Do people have a center of gravity?

Materials:

✓ Handkerchief

Procedure:

1. Stand in the middle of the room. Drop the handkerchief in front of you. Without bending your knees, lean over and pick up the handkerchief.

2. Stand with your back against a wall and try the experiment again. Is it harder this time? Do you lose your balance? Why?

3. Stand in the center of the room and lift your left foot out to the side. Does your body tip slightly to the right to adjust?

4. Try to do the same thing while standing with your right shoulder and foot against a wall. Can you lift your foot now?

WHAT'S HAPPENING HERE?

People have a center of gravity, too. When you are standing still, you are balanced over your center of gravity. If you move a part of your body, without thinking about it, you automatically make other movements to adjust to the new center. When you bend over to pick up the handkerchief, you also shift your weight back a little to stay in balance. With your back against the wall you cannot shift your weight and so you lose your balance.

TEST OF STRENGTH
What is air pressure?

Materials:
- ✓ glass
- ✓ square of smooth cardboard bigger than the rim of the glass

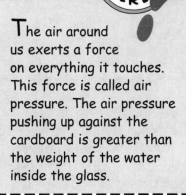

Procedure:

1. Fill the glass with water and cover it with the cardboard. Be sure the cardboard is stiff and flat or the experiment will not work. Hold the cardboard in place with your hand. Standing with your hands over a large sink or bathtub (or outside in the yard) turn the glass over.

2. Remove your hand. What happens? Does the cardboard stay in place? Is the force of the air pushing up greater than the weight of the water?

3. What will happen if you move the cardboard enough to let air into the glass? Try it.

WHAT'S HAPPENING HERE

The air around us exerts a force on everything it touches. This force is called air pressure. The air pressure pushing up against the cardboard is greater than the weight of the water inside the glass.

ROOM FOR CHANGE*

What happens when air is heated or cooled?

Materials:*

- ✓ saucepan
- ✓ quart jar
- ✓ balloon
- ✓ shallow bowl
- ✓ candle about 3 inches tall
- ✓ empty soda bottle
- ✓ marking pen

Procedure:

1. Ask your adult helper to fill a saucepan with very hot water. Slip the neck of the balloon over the rim of the soda bottle and place the bottle in the water. What happens as the air in the bottle heats up? How can you tell?

2. Ask your adult helper to light the candle and drip a little wax into the center of the bowl. Stand the candle up in the wax. Fill the bowl halfway with very cold water. Slowly place the jar upside down over the lit candle and mark the level of the water.

3. Wait until the candle goes out, then lightly touch the side of the jar. Is it warm? Is the air inside warm? After fifteen minutes or so, touch the jar again. Is it cool? Do you think the air inside is cool? Check the water level mark. Is the water higher or lower inside the jar?

WHAT'S HAPPENING HERE?

In the first experiment, when you warm the air inside the bottle it expands or takes up more space. The warm air forced from the bottle goes into the balloon. In the second experiment, you warm the air first, then allow it to cool. As it cools, it contracts or takes up less space. The outside air is pushing down on the water and some is forced up into the jar.

HEAVYWEIGHT
Does air have weight?

Materials:

- ✓ string
- ✓ 2 large balloons
- ✓ light, plastic ruler
- ✓ pin

Procedure:

1. Tie a string in the center of the ruler, then hang it so that it is level.

2. Blow up both balloons to exactly the same size, then tie off the end of each with a piece of string. Hang one balloon from each end of the ruler, adjusting the strings to make the ruler level again so that the balloons are completely balanced.

3. Let the air out of one balloon by bursting it with a pin. What happens to the ruler. Why? What happens if you burst the other balloon?

WHAT'S HAPPENING HERE

Air has weight. With an air-filled balloon on each end of the ruler, it is in balance. If you burst one balloon, the ruler will no longer be in balance and will be pulled down on one side by the weight of the air in the other balloon.

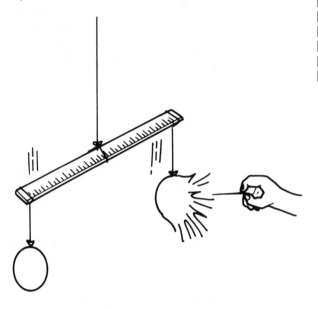

THE EGG AND I*
Can a change in air pressure create a pulling force?

Materials:*

- ✓ 1 small hard-boiled egg
- ✓ baby's milk bottle
- ✓ small piece of paper folded like an accordion
- ✓ cooking oil
- ✓ matches

Procedure:

1. Peel the egg. Rub a little cooking oil on the rim of the bottle.

2. Ask your adult helper to light the paper with a match and drop it into the bottle.

3. Quickly place the egg on top of the bottle. The gas inside will expand and be forced out of the bottle because the egg is not an airtight stopper. What do you think will happen when the air inside the bottle begins to cool? Is the egg pulled into the bottle? How can you get it out?

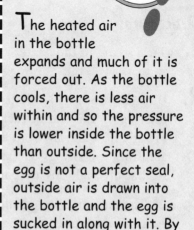

WHAT'S HAPPENING HERE?

The heated air in the bottle expands and much of it is forced out. As the bottle cools, there is less air within and so the pressure is lower inside the bottle than outside. Since the egg is not a perfect seal, outside air is drawn into the bottle and the egg is sucked in along with it. By blowing into the bottle you increase the air pressure inside. There is no longer room for the egg, so it pops out again.

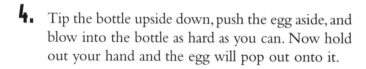

4. Tip the bottle upside down, push the egg aside, and blow into the bottle as hard as you can. Now hold out your hand and the egg will pop out onto it.

34

UP WE GO
How do airplanes stay up in the air?

Materials:

✓ scissors   ✓ notebook paper   ✓ ruler

Procedure:

1. Cut a lengthwise strip from the notebook paper, about two inches wide.

2. Hold the paper in front of you with one of the ends near your mouth. Blow steadily straight ahead and across the top of the strip. What happens to the loose ends?

WHAT'S HAPPENING HERE?

The paper you are holding curves downward. When you blow across it, the air above the paper is moving faster than the air below it. The molecules of the air above the curved surface have a little farther to go than those passing across the flat surface underneath, so they spread out a little and the air also becomes thinner. Because of this, the air pressure is less above than below the paper. The slower, more dense air pushes up with more pressure and the paper moves upward. This is called lift. The wings of an airplane are curved on top to help create lift.

Using Energy and Force

WATER MACHINE*
Can water be made to do work?

Materials:*
- ✓ plastic bottle
- ✓ round file
- ✓ fishing swivel (available at sporting goods stores)
- ✓ scissors
- ✓ string

Procedure:

1. Cut the top of the bottle away. With the scissors, carefully make several holes about one inch apart at the bottom edge of the bottle and two holes at the top edge. File the holes at an angle so that the edges are slightly slanted.

2. Tie a piece of string between the holes at the top. Tie another string at the center of the first. Halfway up the center string, cut and tie in a fishing swivel. Reattach the string at the top of the swivel and tie the loose end to the faucet in the sink. Turn on a stream of water.

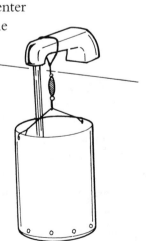

WHAT'S HAPPENING HERE

You have made a water turbine. The water rushes out of the holes at the bottom of the bottle, causing it to turn. It will turn as long as water pours through it. This turbine could move gears and wheels. A turbine in a moving river would be a good source of energy.

ON HOLD
How can stored energy be released?

Materials:
- ✓ a long piece of string
- ✓ a 1-inch wide button

Procedure:

1. Thread the string through both holes in the button. If you are using a button with four holes, thread the string diagonally through two of them only. Tie the loose ends so that you have made a complete loop.

2. Hold the loop outstretched with the button in the middle. Quickly make circles with both hands toward you so that the button spins around and the two rows of string twist together.

3. Pull on both ends of the string. It will untwist and the button will spin in the other direction. When you relax your hold, it will spin back again.

WHAT'S HAPPENING HERE

The button is storing and releasing energy. By pulling on the string, you are supplying more energy, which the button stores and then releases when you relax. You have made something called a flywheel.

POWER BOAT
How can released energy make an object move?

Materials:

- ✓ plastic bottle with screw-on cap
- ✓ drinking straw
- ✓ tissue paper
- ✓ scissors
- ✓ clay
- ✓ ½ cup vinegar
- ✓ 3 tablespoons baking soda

Procedure:

1. Make a hole in the bottom of the bottle, near the edge. Slide the straw into the hole so that only about one inch sticks out. Pack the hole tightly around the straw with clay. Tilt the straw slightly so that it will be underwater when the bottle is placed in water.

2. Put three tablespoons of baking soda in a small square of tissue and roll it to form a tube. Twist both ends tightly shut. Place this in the bottle.

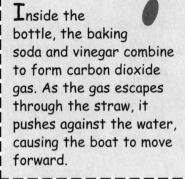

3. Pour one-half cup of vinegar into the bottle, screw on the cap, then set the bottle on its side in a sink about half full of water. Make sure the straw is underwater. What happens? What is causing the boat to move? What happens when it runs out of "fuel"?

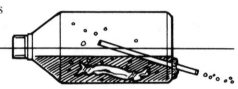

WHAT'S HAPPENING HERE

Inside the bottle, the baking soda and vinegar combine to form carbon dioxide gas. As the gas escapes through the straw, it pushes against the water, causing the boat to move forward.

FIRE THE CANNON
Can expanding gas move an object through air?

Materials:

- ✓ 1 teaspoon baking soda
- ✓ 1/2 cup water
- ✓ 3 pencils
- ✓ 1/2 cup vinegar
- ✓ bottle with cork
- ✓ tissue paper

Procedure:

1. Wrap one teaspoon of baking soda in the tissue paper. Twist the ends to keep it shut. Put this in the bottle and add one-half cup vinegar and one-half cup water. Cork the bottle and wait.

2. What happens to the cork? How far does the cork go? Would it go farther if you used more fuel?

3. Lay the bottle on its side on top of the three pencils. Perform the experiment again. What happens to the bottle when the cork flies out? Why did you need to use the pencils?

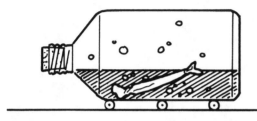

WHAT'S HAPPENING HERE?

In the first experiment, the expanding gas pushes against the cork and forces it out of the bottle. The second part of the experiment is an example of an important scientific law: Every action has an equal and opposite reaction. This means that every time an action takes place (the cork flying from the bottle), an equal but opposite reaction takes place (the bottle rolling backward). We used the pencils to make the reaction more obvious.

PART II

WONDROUS PLANT AND EARTH EXPERIMENTS

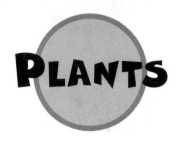

PLANTS

THE SEED
Is the seed useful to plants after they have sprouted?

Materials:

✓ 6 lima beans (frozen or fresh)
✓ glass jar   ✓ blotting paper   ✓ 2 small pots
✓ potting soil   ✓ paper towels   ✓ scissors

Procedure:

1. Soak the lima beans overnight in fresh water.

2. Line the inside of the jar with the blotting paper. Stuff the center with paper towels and fill the jar with water. After a moment, pour out the water. Slip the beans in between the blotting paper and the glass.

3. After the beans sprout (in about one week), carefully remove the young plants and plant three in one pot and three in the other. When the plants are about an inch tall, clip the seeds away from those in one of the pots. Be careful not to clip the leaves. Leave the other three plants as they are. Put both pots in a sunny spot and keep the soil moist.

4. After a week, are the plants different? Do the plants with the seeds look better? Why? Is there something in the seed that the young plant needs?

When most seedbearing plants first sprout, they are unable to use photosynthesis to make food. These young plants get nourishment from the food stored in the seed.

MORE WAYS THAN ONE
Do plants only grow from seeds?

Materials:

- ✓ 2 jars   ✓ knife   ✓ white potato
- ✓ carrot (with some of the green top on it)

Procedure:

1. Cut the carrot about an inch from the top. Fill one of the jars with about one-half inch of water. Place the carrot in the jar, cut side down. What part of the plant does the carrot come from? What do you think will happen?

2. Cut the potato into sections. Be sure that each section has an "eye." Put two or three potato pieces into a glass jar with one-half inch of water in the bottom. What part of the plant does the potato come from?

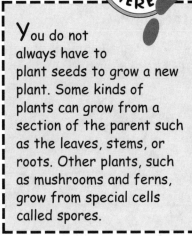

You do not always have to plant seeds to grow a new plant. Some kinds of plants can grow from a section of the parent such as the leaves, stems, or roots. Other plants, such as mushrooms and ferns, grow from special cells called spores.

3. Put both jars in a sunny place. Add water when needed. After two or three days, what happens?

PLANTS FROM SPORES
Where do spores come from?

Materials:

- ✔ 1 can of tomato soup
- ✔ bread crumbs
- ✔ magnifying glass
- ✔ dust
- ✔ 3 small bowls
- ✔ dried leaves
- ✔ plastic wrap

Procedure:

1. Put a small amount of tomato soup in each bowl. Sprinkle bread crumbs in one bowl, place some dried leaves in another, and put some dust (maybe you can find some in a corner of a closet) into the third bowl.

2. Cover each dish with plastic wrap and keep them in a dark closet for three to five days, then examine each. What do you see? The mold growing there are small plants that grew from spores. How did the spores get into the soup? Do you think spores are carried in the air?

3. After two or three more days, examine your mold garden under the magnifying glass. Can you see the tiny plants?

WHAT'S HAPPENING HERE

Tiny spores may float in the air and spread over great distances. They can survive for a long time under unfavorable conditions. When the spores finally come in contact with a substance that enables them to produce new plants, they do.

TAKE A DEEP BREATH
Do plants need air?

Materials:

✓ 2 small green potted plants, 2 or 3 inches tall
✓ 1 pint jar

Procedure:

1. Place both plants side by side in a window that is not in direct sunlight.

2. Put the pint jar upside-down over one plant. Be sure that the jar covers the plant only and not the whole pot. That way you can water the plant without removing the jar and letting any air in.

3. For a few days, care for both plants in the same manner. Keep the soil moist but not wet. What do you think will happen to the plant in the jar?

4. After two or three days, do the plants look different? Which plant is no longer healthy? Why?

5. Remove the jar so that the plant receives a supply of air after a little while. What happens to the plant that was covered? Do plants need air?

WHAT'S HAPPENING HERE?

Green plants need carbon dioxide from the air. Using the energy from sunlight, plants combine carbon dioxide with water to produce the simple sugars the plant uses as food.

45

AIR PASSAGES
How does the air get into the plant?

Materials:

✓ 1 potted green plant with at least 5 or 6 leaves
✓ petroleum jelly

Procedure:

1. Keep the plant in a dark closet for two days.

2. Now put the plant in a sunny spot. Coat one of the leaves on both sides with petroleum jelly. Coat another leaf only on the underside. Put petroleum jelly only on the top of a third leaf. Will the petroleum jelly prevent air from entering the plant?

3. Check the plant after a few days. What has happened to the leaves? Which leaves have dried? Do you think the openings (called stoma) through which plants breathe are located on the top or bottom of the leaf? Why?

There are hundreds of tiny openings called STOMATA in the leaves and sometimes in the stems of green plants. Carbon dioxide enters the plant through these openings.

WATERWAYS
Where does water enter plants?

Materials:
- ✓ 2 small potted green plants
- ✓ aluminum foil   ✓ marking pen

Procedure:

1. Set both plants aside and do not water them for five days.

2. Cover the soil of one pot completely with foil from the stem of the plant to the edge. Mark this pot number one. Tip the pot and run the stem and leaves of the plant under a gentle stream of water. Be sure not to get any water into the soil.

3. Mark the second pot number two and water the plant through the soil as usual.

4. Set both plants in a sunny window. After two days, repeat the watering process. What has happened to the two plants? Do you think plant number one is getting enough water to survive? Why not? Why is plant number two healthier? Where does water enter a plant?

WHAT'S HAPPENING HERE?

Plant roots have many tiny hairlike projections called ROOT HAIRS. Root hairs absorb the water and minerals plants need from the soil.

WHICH WAY?
How does water get from the roots to the leaves?

Materials:

- ✓ red food coloring
- ✓ 2 stalks of celery with leaves
- ✓ glass jar
- ✓ knife
- ✓ pen
- ✓ ruler

Procedure:

1. Fill the jar with water and add a few drops of food coloring. Cut about an inch from the bottom of the celery and put the stalk in water.

2. Check the stalk every half hour. What is happening? Can you see the food coloring traveling inside the stem? If you leave the celery in the jar for a while longer, will the coloring reach the leaves? Try it.

3. Remove the stalk and cut another inch from the bottom. The small circles you see are the ends of fluid-filled tubes that run the length of the plant. These tubes are what carry the water to the leaves. The water in the tubes also keeps the plant stem firm.

4. Pour out the colored water and wash the jar. Place the second stalk of celery in direct sunlight for a few hours. What happened to the water in the celery? Without water to support the stems how is the celery different?

5. Fill the jar with fresh cool water and place the stalk in it. Leave it for an hour or so. Is the celery any different? Why?

WHAT'S HAPPENING HERE?

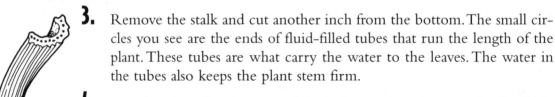

Tiny tubes, called XYLEM (zi-lem), in the stems and leaves of a green plant transport the water from the roots. Water is drawn up from the roots and carried to every part of the plant where it is needed. The water inside the xylem also helps to support the plant and keep it firm.

WAY OUT
How does the water leave a plant?

Materials:
- ✓ small plastic bag
- ✓ twist ties
- ✓ potted geranium

Procedure:

1. Put the plastic bag over several leaves and tie it off near the stem as close to the soil as possible.

2. Leave the plant in a sunny window for two or three hours. What happens?

3. Open the bag. What is inside? Where did the water come from? So do you think the leaves that are not covered are also releasing water into the air?

WHAT'S HAPPENING HERE?

Not all of the water taken in by a plant is used in the process of photosynthesis. In most green, leafy plants excess water seeps out through the stomata. The stomata are tiny openings—not visible by the naked eye—which are located in the epidermise of the plant leaves. This process is called TRANSPIRATION.

TURN ON THE LIGHTS
Do plants need light?

Materials:

- ✓ 4 potted plants
- ✓ stapler
- ✓ petroleum jelly
- ✓ white paper

Procedure:

1. Mark one plant number one and put it in a closet out of the light. Mark another plant number two and put it in a sunny window. For three or four days, care for each plant in the same way. What happens? Does the soil in one stay wetter? Which one? Does one plant look better than the other? Why?

2. Move the sick plant into the light. Do you think it will recover?

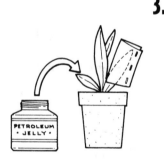

3. On plant number two, coat the top of one leaf with petroleum jelly so nothing but light can enter. Staple a piece of paper around another leaf on the same plant. Which leaf will do better? Why?

4. Mark the last two plants three and four. Keep both in a closet. Expose one to light for a few hours only in the morning. Give the other plant light only in the afternoon. Is there a difference?

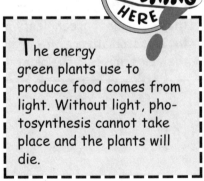

WHAT'S HAPPENING HERE

The energy green plants use to produce food comes from light. Without light, photosynthesis cannot take place and the plants will die.

TOWARD THE LIGHT
Do plant leaves always grow upward?

Materials:
- ✓ 6 fresh lima beans
- ✓ blotting paper
- ✓ large glass jar
- ✓ paper towels

Procedure:

1. Begin by soaking the beans overnight in water.

2. The following day, line the inside of the jar with blotting paper. Stuff paper towels into the center and fill it with water. Wait five minutes, then drain off the water.

3. Put the beans between the blotting paper and the jar. Place each one at a different angle. Keep the jar in a closet for two to three days. Be sure to keep the blotting paper and paper towels moist so that the beans will sprout. Since the beans are all in different angles, will the stems grow in different directions?

4. Observe the jar after two or three days. Did you guess correctly? Turn the jar on its side and wait a day or two before you check it again. What happens to the roots and stems now?

WHAT'S HAPPENING HERE

There are hormones in the tips of plant roots that are sensitive to the Earth's gravitational pull and cause the roots to grow downward. Hormones in the tip of the stem are sensitive to light. That is why plants will grow toward a sunny window. This reaction is called TROPISM.

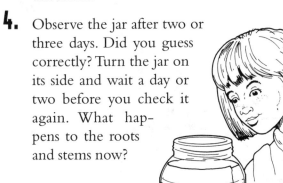

MEAL TIME
Do all plants use photosynthesis to make food?

Materials:
- ✓ 2 large glass jars with lids
- ✓ 2 1-foot-long pieces of rubber tubing
- ✓ 1 package of baker's yeast (a simple plant)
- ✓ measuring cup   ✓ measuring spoon   ✓ sugar   ✓ 2 clothespins
- ✓ marking pen   ✓ 2 glasses   ✓ flour

Procedure:

1. Punch a hole in one of the jar lids large enough to slip in the tubing. Seal the hole with a ball of clay.

2. Mix one cup of flour with one tablespoon of sugar, one-quarter package of yeast, and one-half cup of water. Knead this into a dough and put it in the bottom of the jar with the hole in the lid. Mark this jar number one. Screw on the lid tightly.

3. Mix another batch of dough for the second jar marked number two, but this time leave out the sugar. Place both jars in a warm spot.

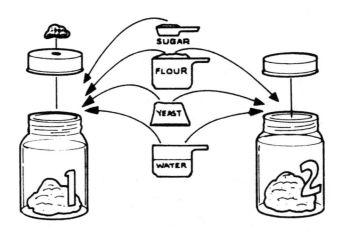

4. Check the jars after two hours. What has happened? Did the dough behave differently in one jar than the other? What was different about the preparation? What was the food consumed by the active yeast?

5. What caused the bread to rise? Fill a glass with limewater. Remove the lid from jar number one. Remove the clay, slip in the tube, and pack clay around the edges. Clip the end of the tube shut with a clothespin.

6. Puncture several holes in the dough and rapidly replace the lid. Remove the clothespin from the tube and, as quickly as you can, place the open end of the tube in the glass of limewater. If the limewater turns milky, then the gas carbon dioxide is present. What happens?

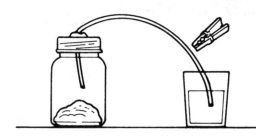

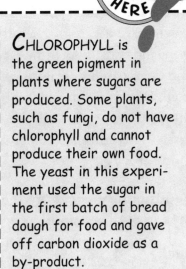

WHAT'S HAPPENING HERE

CHLOROPHYLL is the green pigment in plants where sugars are produced. Some plants, such as fungi, do not have chlorophyll and cannot produce their own food. The yeast in this experiment used the sugar in the first batch of bread dough for food and gave off carbon dioxide as a by-product.

Rocks, Soil, and Minerals

When Earth formed about 4.5 billion years ago, it was a swirling ball of molten rock. Eventually it cooled and hardened, forming a thin crust called the LITHOSPHERE. The crust is made up of rocks and minerals. Minerals are non-living substances that occur naturally in the Earth, have a certain chemical composition, and usually form in crystals. Calcite and quartz are minerals, as are copper and gold. Rocks are usually combinations of minerals, but some may be made up of just one type. There are three different kinds of rocks.

Sedimentary rocks are the most common type. They form over millions of years, when tiny particles from minerals, plant, and animals are pressed and cemented together. Limestone, sandstone, and coal are sedimentary rocks.

Sandstone
(Sedimentary)

Igneous rocks form when molten magma (rock material) from deep within the Earth cools and hardens. Granite and basalt are examples of igneous rocks.

Granite
(Igneous)

Metamorphic rocks are those that are changed from one type of rock to another usually by great heat and pressure. Marble is an example of metamorphic rock, which is formed from limestone.

Slate
(Metamorphic)

54

HARDNESS
How hard is rock?

Materials:

- ✓ penny
- ✓ steel file
- ✓ nail
- ✓ blackboard chalk
- ✓ tailor's chalk (or talc)
- ✓ pencil lead (graphite)
- ✓ emery paper
- ✓ notebook

Procedure:

1. Some rocks, minerals, and their products are harder than others. To test this, you must make a scale of hardness. Scientists use a scale called Mohs's scale, which grades various minerals from one to ten. You can make your own scale.

2. Begin with the penny. Use it to try to scratch the other objects. Put the things that can be scratched by the penny on one side, and those that cannot on the other side.

3. From one pile, select an object and test it against the others in the pile. Some will be harder. Some will be softer. Continue to do this until each object has a place in line, harder than the neighbor on one side and softer than the neighbor on the other.

4. Assign the first object, probably the tailor's chalk, number one. Each object gets a number according to its place in line. Record your results in the notebook. Now you have made a scale to test other objects against. What will you name your scale?

WHAT'S HAPPENING HERE

The hardness of a substance depends on how close the atoms in the substance are to each other and how strongly they are attracted to each other. If the attraction is weak, the material is more easily scratched.

CRYSTALS
How do crystals form?

Materials:

- ✓ tall glass jar
- ✓ spoon
- ✓ sugar
- ✓ food coloring
- ✓ paper clip
- ✓ pencil
- ✓ 1 foot of light string

Procedure:

1. Fill the jar with very hot water. Stir in sugar, a spoonful at a time, until no more will dissolve in the water. Add a few drops of food coloring.

2. Tie one end of the string around the middle of the pencil and attach the paper clip to the other end. Lower the string into the jar. Turn the pencil to shorten the string until the paper clip hangs an inch from the bottom.

3. Let the jar set for a few days. Crystals will form. The longer you wait, the larger the crystals will grow. Are the crystals made of sugar? Taste them. This is how rock candy is made. Crystals can be made from salt, too.

When certain substances form, the atoms become arranged in an orderly pattern. This pattern is the CRYSTAL STRUCTURE. As more atoms are attracted and join this structure, the crystal "grows." Crystals form in one of two ways, evaporation or cooling. By stirring the sugar into hot water you break down the crystals. As the water cools, the crystals reform.

BENEATH YOUR FEET
What is soil made of?

Materials:

- ✓ 6 glass jars with lids
- ✓ marking pen
- ✓ small spade
- ✓ magnifying glass
- ✓ 6 stick-on labels
- ✓ siphon
- ✓ kitchen bulb
- ✓ soil

Procedure:

1. Fill each jar with three inches of soil, each sample collected from a different place. Put a label on the jars and write the place where the sample was collected. Note the type of plants that were growing in the soil and any other interesting characteristics. Were there any animals living in the soil?

2. When all the samples have been collected, fill each jar with water and shake well. What happens to the water? Allow each sample to settle. Check them every hour. The contents of which jar settled first? Did the soil form layers? The heaviest elements in the soil will have settled first and will be on the bottom.

3. Siphon out as much water as possible, then set the jars in a sunny spot. The rest of the water will evaporate.

4. When the soil has dried, take a sample from each layer to examine under the magnifying glass. How is each layer different? Do they feel different? Is soil made up of a combination of things?

WHAT'S HAPPENING HERE?

Soil is formed from weathered rock and minerals. The type of soil depends on a number of things, including the original rock, the climate, and the plants that were in the area as the soil formed.

SOGGY SOIL
Which holds more water, sandy soil or clay soil?

Materials:
- ✓ 2 paper cups
- ✓ clay soil
- ✓ sandy soil
- ✓ 2 measuring cups

Procedure:

1. Make a small hole in the bottom of each cup. Fill one cup with sandy soil and the other with clay soil.

2. Fill one measuring cup to half full with water. Hold the paper cup filled with clay soil over the empty measuring cup and pour the water over the soil. Wait until it stops draining. Note how much water poured through.

3. Repeat the procedure, this time with sandy soil. Which one held the most water? Do you think that different kinds of plants need different kinds of soil? Do plants that need little water grow best in sandy or clay soil? Why?

EROSION

DISAPPEARING SOIL*
Does rain erode soil?

Materials:*
- ✓ hammer
- ✓ pebbles
- ✓ nail
- ✓ cookie tin
- ✓ coffee can
- ✓ clay
- ✓ newspaper
- ✓ soil

Procedure:

1. Have a parent help you. With the hammer and the nail, punch many small holes in the bottom of the coffee can. Spread the newspaper on a flat surface out of doors. Put a layer of pebbles in the bottom of the cookie tin and top it with a layer of soil. Place the cookie tin on the newspaper so that it is slightly tilted.

2. Hold the coffee can over the cookie tin. Pour the water into the can. Let it rain down on the slope you have created. What happens to the soil? What is left if you continue to pour rain on the slope? Can rainwater cause soil erosion?

3. Set up your slope again but this time, before you add the soil, place several balls of clay on the tray to hold artificial plants in place. Fill the tray with soil, push the plant stems into the clay, and provide rain.

4. Is there less soil erosion when plants are on the slope? Would a layer of grass hold the soil in place? During a heavy rainfall, what would happen to a hillside on which a fire has destroyed the plants and grass?

59

CRACKED ROCKS*
Can temperature changes cause erosion?

Materials:*
- ✓ clear plastic jar
- ✓ tongs
- ✓ pot holder
- ✓ small rock
- ✓ balloon
- ✓ bowl
- ✓ rubber gloves
- ✓ newspapers
- ✓ notebook
- ✓ magnifying glass
- ✓ plaster of Paris

Procedure:

1. Erosion is the wearing away of rocks and soil. Fill the jar with cool water. Ask your adult helper to use the tongs to hold a small rock over an open flame until it is very hot. Put the rock into the cool water. What happens? Examine the rock with the magnifying glass. Do cracks form?

2. Fill the balloon with water and tie it closed.

3. Wearing rubber gloves, make a thick plaster of Paris mixture in the bowl according to directions. Form a ball around the balloon several layers thick. Put the balloon on the newspaper so that you don't make a big mess.

4. Place the covered balloon in the freezer overnight. What happened when the water in the balloon froze? What would happen if rainwater filled a crack in a rock and froze?

Wind can also cause erosion. So can pollution. Walk around your neighborhood and look for examples of erosion. Keep a list in your notebook of the type of erosion you find and what might have caused it.

Generally, heat causes things to expand and cold causes things to contract. The rapid heating and cooling of a material weakens it and it may crack. This may happen to rocks in a desert that bake by day and become very cold at night. Water is the only material that expands when it freezes. If water freezes in a crack, it can put tremendous pressure on this already weak point in the rock.

CARVING CAVES
How are caves formed?

Materials:

- ✓ measuring cup
- ✓ 2 pieces of granite
- ✓ saucepan
- ✓ bottle of plain soda water
- ✓ 2 pieces of limestone (available at rock shops or garden supply stores)
- ✓ spoon
- ✓ marking pen
- ✓ 2 glass jars

WHAT'S HAPPENING HERE?

CALCITE is a form of calcium carbonate. Limestone is made up mostly of calcite. Rainwater becomes slightly acidic as it seeps through the soil. It can slowly dissolve underground calcite deposits, leaving caverns.

Procedure:

1. Boil two cups of water in a saucepan to purify it. Let the water cool, then pour it into one of the jars. Mark the jar number one.

2. Fill a jar marked number two with soda water. Stir the soda water until the bubbles are gone. Let it set for a while, then stir again.

3. Put a piece of limestone and a piece of granite in each jar. What happens? How are the reactions different? The soda water in jar two is slightly acidic. It reacts with the calcite and will finally dissolve it. Do you think there is calcite in the granite?

4. How can rainwater affect areas made up of granite and limestone?

WATER SCULPTURE
How do stalactites form in caves?

Materials:

- ✓ 2 glass jars
- ✓ spoon
- ✓ small plate
- ✓ pot holders
- ✓ Epsom salts
- ✓ 8 inches of heavy wool knitting yarn

Procedure:

1. Have a parent help you fill both jars with very hot water. Stir in Epsom salts one spoonful at a time, until the water can hold no more.

2. Place the jars where they will not be disturbed. Put the small plate between them, and put one end of the wool yarn in each jar. After three or four days, check your experiment. What is happening? What is your stalagmite made of? Will the columns on the bottom and top eventually meet? Try it.

WHAT'S HAPPENING HERE?

The water and dissolved Epsom salts in the jars are absorbed by the wool. As the water collects in the center of the strand, it will begin to drip very slowly. As each drop hangs from the wool, the water begins to evaporate leaving behind the salts, which build up after a while. Some drops may fall to the plate and a salt formation will grow there, too. It is through this same process that cones and columns form in caves. A STALACTITE forms on the roof of a cave. The formation on the floor of a cave is a STALAGMITE.

ROCKS FROM LIVING THINGS
Do all rocks and minerals contain carbonates?

Materials:

- ✓ file
- ✓ baking soda
- ✓ eggshell
- ✓ bowl
- ✓ different kinds of rocks

- ✓ hammer
- ✓ real chalk
- ✓ seashell
- ✓ eyedropper

- ✓ limestone
- ✓ marble
- ✓ salt
- ✓ vinegar

Procedure:

1. Certain rocks—chalk, for instance—are made up of the remains, such as shells, of living creatures. (Blackboard chalk is usually made up of another material called gypsum. Real chalk can be obtained from a paint store.) These rocks and some other rocks and minerals contain carbonates.

2. To find out if there are carbonates in a material, file a small portion of the object you are testing or crack it with a hammer. If possible, crush the object or a piece of it and place it in the bowl.

3. Using the eyedropper, drop several drops of vinegar on the material you are testing. What happens? Does it fizz or bubble? If so, the object contains carbonates. Test the other materials, such as baking soda, marble, and salt.

WHAT'S HAPPENING HERE

The bubbling is caused when carbonates come in contact with a weak acid, such as vinegar, and carbon dioxide is released.

WATER

Living things on Earth need water to survive. More than 70 percent of the surface of our planet is covered by water, which makes up the HYDROSPHERE.

Most of this is salt water in the oceans and seas. Another 2 percent is frozen into the ice and snow of Earth's polar regions. The rest is fresh water in lakes and rivers, groundwater, and vapor in the air.

HEAVY WATER
Which is heavier, fresh or salt water?

Materials:
- ✓ 2 pop bottles
- ✓ 3 x 5 card
- ✓ measuring spoons
- ✓ food coloring
- ✓ salt

Procedure:

1. Fill one bottle with water, add three teaspoons of salt, and shake it. Fill the second bottle with water. Add some food coloring to this bottle.

2. Place the 3 x 5 card over the opening of the bottle containing salty water. Hold the card in place with your hand and turn over the bottle.

3. Balance this bottle on top of the one containing fresh water. Carefully slip the card out from between. What happens? The heaviest solution will drift to the bottom. Is the salt water heavier?

DENSITY is the ratio of weight to volume. If two substances are of the same volume but one is more dense, the denser substance will be heavier. Seawater is more dense because in each volume of water there is the weight of the water plus the additional weight of the dissolved salts.

SALTY RAIN
Why doesn't water from the ocean fall as salty rain?

Materials:

- ✓ measuring cup
- ✓ glass pint jar
- ✓ large plastic trash bag
- ✓ large tub at least 6 inches high
- ✓ salt
- ✓ small rock
- ✓ spoon
- ✓ tape

Procedure:

1. Fill the tub with three inches of water, pour in one-half cup of salt, enough to make the water taste salty. Put the tub where it will be in direct sunlight for most of the day.

2. Set the jar in the center of the tub. Cover the top of the tub completely with the plastic trash bag. Tape the bag in place. Put the rock in the center so that it weights the plastic down toward the glass. The bag must not touch the glass. What will happen as the water heats up?

3. As the water evaporates, it cannot escape but instead will condense on the plastic and flow toward the glass. Does salt evaporate in sunlight? Will there be salt water in the glass or fresh water?

4. At the end of the day, take out the glass and taste the water. Did you answer correctly? Where is the salt? Why?

WHAT'S HAPPENING HERE?

As it warms, the water in the tub evaporates, leaving the salt behind.

DEEP WATER
Is deep ocean water usually warmer or colder than water at the surface?

Materials:
- ✓ empty ice tray
- ✓ food coloring
- ✓ rubber band
- ✓ 1 quart glass jar with a wide mouth
- ✓ 2 feet of string
- ✓ small glass bottle

Procedure Part One:

1. Fill the ice tray with water tinted with several drops of food coloring. Freeze it overnight.

2. Fill the quart jar with luke warm water.

3. Add two or three colored ice cubes. What happens as the ice melts? Does the cold water form a layer?

Procedure Part Two:

1. Fill the quart jar with very cold water.

2. Loop the rubber band around the lip of the small bottle. Tie each end of the string to the rubber band so that the bottle can be lifted without tilting.

3. Fill the small bottle with hot water and add a few drops of food coloring.

4. Lower the bottle carefully by the string into the jar of cold water. What happens? Can you see swirls of colored water rising from the bottle? Does the warm colored water mix with the rest of the water? Where does the warm water go?

WHAT'S HAPPENING HERE

The molecules in cold water are more closely packed than the molecules in warm water. Because of this, cold water is more dense and will usually sink, while less dense warm water will rise. In general, deep ocean water is colder than the water at the surface.

67

FREEZING POINT
Does ocean and fresh water freeze at the same temperature?

Materials:

✓ 2 plastic margarine containers   ✓ marking pen
✓ measuring spoons   ✓ thermometer   ✓ salt

Procedure:

1. Mark one container number one and fill it with water.

2. Mark the second container number two. Fill it with water. Stir two teaspoons of salt into the water. Record the temperature of the water in each container, then put both in the freezer.

WHAT'S HAPPENING HERE

Pure water freezes at 32° Fahrenheit. Water with dissolved salts does not freeze until 28.6° Fahrenheit. Sodium and chlorine are the two most plentiful elements in seawater. They combine to make sodium chloride or common salt.

3. Check the temperature of each container of water every hour. Which container freezes first? Which has a lower freezing point?

FLOATING ICE
Why do icebergs float?

Materials:

✓ 1 plastic margarine container with lid
✓ measuring spoons   ✓ 2 glass bowls
✓ tray of ice   ✓ salt

Procedure:

1. Fill the margarine container to the rim with water. Put the lid on the container and freeze it overnight. Does the ice take up more or less room than the same amount of water? Do you think ice is lighter or heavier than the same amount of water?

2. Fill one bowl with fresh water. Fill the second bowl with water, add two teaspoons of salt, and stir.

3. Place an ice cube in each bowl. Look very carefully. Does the ice cube in the salt water float slightly higher than the cube in fresh water? Why? Why do icebergs float in the ocean? Can the lower freezing point of salt water help an iceberg to last longer?

WHAT'S HAPPENING HERE

When water freezes, the molecules line up in such a way that there is more space between them than when they are in liquid form. The ice expands and takes up more space. For this reason, the same volume of ice weighs less than the same volume of water.

WEATHER

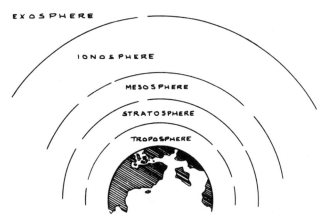

EXOSPHERE

IONOSPHERE

MESOSPHERE

STRATOSPHERE

TROPOSPHERE

Protective gases, mostly nitrogen and oxygen, surround Earth and make up the ATMOSPHERE. The atmosphere includes four main layers and a thin outer layer.

The **exosphere** is the very thin outermost layer.

The **ionosphere** is between thirty and three hundred miles above Earth. Temperatures here can very from -1120° Fahrenheit at lower levels to more than 2500° Fahrenheit.

Mesosphere: a layer of the atmosphere extending from the top of the stratosphere to an altitude of about 50 miles.

The **stratosphere** lies between thirty miles to about ten miles above Earth's surface. Within this area of the atmosphere is the protective *ozone layer* that absorbs dangerous radiation from the Sun.

The **troposphere** is the layer nearest Earth. It holds most of the planet's water vapor. Within the troposphere are strong, high-level winds called *jet streams* that have much influence on Earth's climates and on changeable weather.

MOVING AIR*
What is wind?

Materials:*
- ✓ 2 balloons
- ✓ small pan
- ✓ scissors
- ✓ padded glove
- ✓ 2 pop bottles
- ✓ white paper
- ✓ pencil
- ✓ candle

Procedure:

1. Warm air rises. To demonstrate this, slip a balloon over the rim of each empty pop bottle.

2. Fill the pan with hot water and place one bottle in the water. What happens to the balloon? Why? What happens to the balloon that is not in the warm water? Why?

3. Here is another way to show that warm air rises. Draw a spiral shape on a piece of paper and cut it out. Place the end of the spiral over the pencil tip. Light the candle, and wearing the padded glove, hold the pencil above the candle. What happens to the paper spiral? Why?

WHAT'S HAPPENING HERE

Warm air rises. By putting the pop bottle in the hot water you are heating the air inside. Wind is the movement of air. One cause of this movement is the uneven heating of the atmosphere by the Sun. As the warm air rises, cooler air moves in to take its place. This may be felt as wind.

CHILLY MEETING
Does cold air sink?

Materials:

- ✓ 6 to 8 ice cubes
- ✓ measuring spoons
- ✓ twist tie
- ✓ 2 pencils
- ✓ plastic bag
- ✓ salt
- ✓ thermometer
- ✓ oatmeal box

Procedure:

1. Lightly crush the ice and put it in the plastic bag. Add one teaspoon of salt and seal the bag.

2. Make a small hole in the bottom of the oatmeal box and insert the thermometer. Note the temperature of the air in the box.

3. Put the pencils across the open top of the box and rest the bag of ice on them. Wait fifteen minutes and read the temperature again. Is it cooler? Why? Does the warm air begin to cool as it passes the ice?

WHAT'S HAPPENING HERE?

Cool air, being more dense, is heavier than warm air. Even though the ice is not in the box, the cooler air around it will sink and the temperature in the box will lower.

STICKY WEATHER
Why are hot, humid days more uncomfortable than hot, dry days?

Materials:

- ✓ glass
- ✓ thermometer
- ✓ blotting paper
- ✓ paper towels
- ✓ twist tie

Procedure:

1. Fill the glass with water that is the same temperature as the room. Tear a small strip from the paper towel, dip it in the water, and wrap it around the bulb of the thermometer. Hold the strip in place with the twist tie. Record the temperature. Has it changed?

2. Put the thermometer in the glass of water and record the temperature after five minutes.

3. Line the glass with a piece of blotting paper. Wait a moment, then pour out the water. In the air of the room, wrapping the thermometer in a moist towel made the temperature drop. Will the same thing happen in the moisture-filled air in the glass? Try it.

WHAT'S HAPPENING HERE?

Water vapor in the air is called HUMIDITY. The evaporation of water from your skin as sweat has a cooling effect, but the air can only hold a certain amount of water. When humidity is high sweat will stay on your skin and you will feel sticky and uncomfortable.

FOG IN A BOTTLE
How does fog form?

Materials:

- ✓ 1 ice cube
- ✓ potholders
- ✓ plastic wrap
- ✓ clear glass pop or juice bottle

Procedure:

1. Wearing the potholders, fill the bottle with hot water. Let it set for a moment. Pour out most of the water leaving about an inch in the bottle.

2. Put the ice cube on top of the bottle. What happens as the warm, moist air meets the cold air?

3. Cover the ice in plastic wrap and repeat the experiment. Did the fog appear? Is the water vapor from which the fog forms in the ice or in the warm air?

WHAT'S HAPPENING HERE?

The warm air in the bottle holds water vapor. It is cooled when it comes in contact with the ice. The water vapor condenses onto particles in the air, forming tiny droplets that you see as fog.

DEW POINT
At what temperature will water vapor condense?

Materials:

- ✓ shiny metal coffee can
- ✓ thermometer
- ✓ paper towel
- ✓ 6 to 8 ice cubes

Procedure:

1. Fill the can three-quarters full with water. Carefully dry the outside of the can.

2. Stirring with the thermometer, add the ice one cube at a time. Allow each ice cube to melt before adding the next. Note the temperature when drops begin to form on the outside of the can. Where does the water on the outside come from? The temperature at which water vapor condenses is called the dew point.

3. Do you think the dew point is always the same? Repeat this experiment on several different days. Compare the temperatures. Try the experiment on a cloudy day or at night. Does this make a difference?

WHAT'S HAPPENING HERE

As air becomes cool, it is unable to hold as much water vapor as warm air. The air around the can is slowly cooled to the point that the water condenses and droplets form on the chilled surface of the can.

APRIL SHOWERS*
How does rain form?

Materials:*

✓ metal pot ✓ metal pie pan ✓ 12 ice cubes ✓ padded glove ✓ marking pen

Procedure:

1. Fill the pot with water and bring it to a steady boil. Can you see the water vapor rising into the air?

2. Fill the pie pan with ice and some water. Wearing the padded glove to protect your hand, hold the pie pan about six inches above the pot. What happens to the water vapor when it touches the bottom of the pan? Why?

3. The droplets on the pie pan will fall when they become heavy enough. What happens to water vapor carried upward in currents of warm air? Where does water vapor in the air come from?

4. Remove the ice cubes from the pie pan. Mark the level of the water in the pan and place it in a sunny window for a few days. What happens? Is the water level lower? Where has it gone?

WHAT'S HAPPENING HERE

When warm air encounters the very cold air of the upper atmosphere, water vapor condenses onto smoke or dust particles and freezes into small ice crystals. As the ice crystals collect, clouds develop. When the crystals become too heavy they begin to fall back to Earth. If the temperature is low enough, they will fall as snow or hail. Usually they melt in the warmer lower atmosphere and fall as rain.

WHAT GOES UP MUST COME DOWN*
What is the rain cycle?

Materials:*
- ✓ 3 small potted plants
- ✓ hot plate
- ✓ padded glove
- ✓ 2 metal cookie trays
- ✓ teakettle
- ✓ 12 ice cubes

Procedure:

1. Place the plants on one tray next to the hot plate. Fill the teakettle with water, place it on the hot plate, and bring it to a boil with the spout facing toward the tray.

2. Fill the second tray with ice and some water. Hold it above the plants and close enough to the teakettle so that vapor will reach it.

3. The teakettle represents the source of the water vapor, such as an ocean or lake. The upper tray is cold air in the atmosphere. What will happen as the water vapor condenses? What will finally happen to the water that has fallen on the small plants as rain?

Water is constantly evaporating from the surface of Earth's great bodies of water. The water vapor is carried by warm air high into the upper atmosphere. At this point, the air cools, the water vapor condenses, and, when conditions are right, it falls as rain. Some of the rainwater may be absorbed by plants and released back into the air through transpiration. (Transpiration is the passage of water vapor from a living body.) Most of it finds its way to streams, rivers, lakes, and oceans, and the cycle begins again.

77

YOUR WEATHER STATION

The most important thing to do is to keep good records. Take daily readings of temperature. Note cloud and wind conditions and look for weather patterns. Here are a few instruments you will need in your weather station.

THE WIND VANE (used to tell wind direction)*

Materials:*
- ✓ thin board
- ✓ hammer
- ✓ compass
- ✓ 1 piece of wood, 6 inches long by 1/2 inch wide
- ✓ 1 piece of wood, 1 inch square and 1 foot long
- ✓ small handsaw
- ✓ drill
- ✓ 2-inch headless nail
- ✓ glass eyedropper
- ✓ marking pen
- ✓ tongs
- ✓ glue

Procedure:

1. Make a small slit about one inch deep in each end of the six-inch piece of wood. From the thin board, cut shapes that look like those in the illustration, then slip them into the slots and glue them securely.

2. Seal the small end of the eyedropper by turning it over a low flame. Hold the glass with tongs so that you don't burn your fingers.

3. Drive the nail into the top of the foot-long piece of wood. Find the spot on your arrow at which it will balance on the nail without falling. Mark that spot and drill a small hole there a little wider than the end of the eyedropper.

4. Slip the eyedropper over the nail and insert the other end into the hole in the arrow. It should spin freely. Mount your wind vane in an open area. Aim your compass in the direction the arrow is pointing to determine the direction of the wind.

THE BAROMETER (used to gauge air pressure)

Materials:

- ✓ 1 balloon
- ✓ large jar
- ✓ glue
- ✓ 3 x 5 card
- ✓ scissors
- ✓ rubber band
- ✓ 1 plastic straw
- ✓ marking pen

Procedure:

1. Cut a section from the balloon. Stretch it over the top of the jar using the rubber band to hold it in place. Put a drop of glue in the center of the balloon. Attach the straw horizontally by one end.

2. Put the jar on a tabletop near a wall. Pin the white card to the wall next to the jar. Write the word high above the level of the straw. When the air pressure is high, it will push down on the balloon causing the straw "indicator" to point to high.

THE NEPHOSCOPE (used to determine how fast and from what direction the wind is blowing high above the Earth)

Materials:
- ✓ measuring tape
- ✓ mirror, 6 inches in diameter
- ✓ paintbrush
- ✓ stopwatch
- ✓ piece of cardboard, 8 inches in diameter
- ✓ compass
- ✓ glue
- ✓ white paint

Procedure:

1. Glue the mirror in the center of the cardboard so that there is an even border all the way around it. Use the measuring tape to find the center of the mirror and put a dot of white paint there. On the border, write an *N* for north, an *S* for south, and so on, as shown in the example.

2. Put your nethoscope on a flat surface outside. Use the compass to be sure that the *N* is facing directly north. As a cloud passes across the mirror, note from which direction it has come.

3. Use a stopwatch, or a watch with a second hand, to time how long it takes for the edge of the cloud to travel across the mirror.

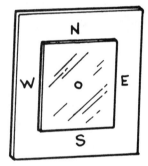

The Sun and the Moon

EARTH'S NEIGHBORS
Why does the Moon have phases?

Materials:

- ✓ knitting needle
- ✓ tennis ball
- ✓ lamp

Procedure:

1. Push the knitting needle into the ball to use as a handle.

2. Place the lamp on a table in a darkened room. Stand about three feet away from it. Hold the ball by the needle slightly above your head so that the light falls on it. You represent Earth. The lamp is the Sun, and the tennis ball is the Moon. Stand with your back to the light. The tennis ball is completely lit. Now slowly turn in a circle watching the ball. How does it change? What happens when you are facing the lamp?

3. What would happen if you (Earth) were to pass between the Sun and the Moon? Try it. The darkening of the Moon in this manner is called a lunar eclipse. What do you think would happen if the Moon moved between your view from Earth of the Sun? Solar eclipses are not visible to everyone on Earth at the same time. Why not?

WHAT'S HAPPENING HERE?

Half of the Moon is always lit by the Sun. The Moon takes about thirty days to orbit around Earth. We see different amounts of the sunlit portion of the Moon depending on its position in orbit around us.

PERMANENT ICE
Why don't the polar ice caps melt away?

Materials:

- ✓ black paint
- ✓ paintbrush
- ✓ thermometer
- ✓ white paint
- ✓ 2 coffee cans

Procedure:

1. Paint the outside of one can black, the other white. Fill both cans with water.

2. Place both cans in the Sun and record the temperature of the water. An hour later, which can do you think will contain hotter water?

3. Test it. Which one was hotter? Bright surfaces reflect heat while dark surfaces absorb it. Would a field of bright snow absorb or reflect the warm rays of the Sun?

WHAT'S HAPPENING HERE?

The rate at which a surface reflects light is called its ALBEDO. Dark surfaces have a low albedo while bright snow has a very high albedo. Instead of being absorbed, much of the heat radiation that can cause the temperature to rise is reflected away. The longer the ice field, the greater this effect becomes. Of course, some of the ice and snow melts and the ice caps become smaller in summer, but they never melt away completely.

RED SKY AT NIGHT
Why is the sky at sunset sometimes red?

Materials:

✓ glass jar ✓ flashlight ✓ milk

Procedure:

1. Fill the glass jar with water. In a darkened room, hold the flashlight level with the center of the glass jar and shine the light into the water. What color does the water appear? The water is scattering the light and reflecting blue light to your eye. The same thing happens when light is scattered by the atmosphere. That is why the sky looks blue during the day.

2. Now move so that you are on the opposite side of the glass jar from the flashlight. Does the color change when you are looking at the light through the water?

3. Pour some milk into the glass jar. Look at the water from the same side as the flashlight. Does it appear blue again?

4. Move so that you are once again looking at the light through the water. Now what color do you see?

WHAT'S HAPPENING HERE

The milk represents dust and water vapor in the atmosphere. When the Sun is low on the horizon, its light falls at a different angle and often only the red light reaches your eye.

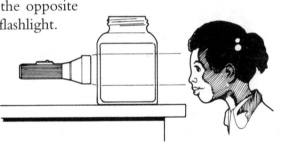

THE FOUR SEASONS
Why are there seasons on Earth?

Materials:

- ✓ marking pen
- ✓ knitting needle
- ✓ tennis ball
- ✓ lamp

Procedure:

1. Draw a line around the middle of the ball to represent the equator. Put a large dot on the equator. Put another dot an inch above the first and one an inch below the first. These dots represent cities. Push the knitting needle through the top of the ball and out the other side. This is Earth's axis.

2. Put the lamp in the center of a darkened room. Stand about two feet away from the lamp. With one end of the knitting needle, hold the ball even with the bulb.

3. Earth is slightly tilted on its axis about twenty-three degrees. Hold your hand so that your index finger points straight up. Spread your fingers as wide as you can. The space between your index and ring fingers is about twenty-three degrees. Hold the needle so that it is at the same angle as your ring finger pointing away from the lamp. Be sure your cities are facing the light. This position represents Earth on December 22nd. Which city is getting the most light? Which city do you think is the coldest at this time of year?

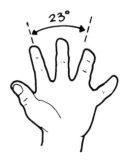

84

4. Move one quarter of the way around the light. Rotate the ball so that cities continue to face the light and the angle is the same as in the illustration. Which city is becoming warmer? Continue another quarter trip around the lamp. Now the needle faces the Sun. Which city is the warmest? What season do you think it is in that city? Move another quarter turn. Now what is happening? What would happen if Earth's axis was not tilted? Does winter occur at the same time of year above and below the equator?

If Earth was not tilted on its axis, there would be no difference in the seasons. Because of the tilt, areas tilted toward the Sun have longer periods of daylight and the rays of the Sun are more direct. As Earth moves in its orbit around the Sun, the same areas become tilted away from the Sun. They then have shorter periods of daylight. The Sun's rays reach them at more of a slant and are not as strong.

GLOSSARY
Science Words You Should Know

animal   a living thing that is capable of reproduction and is not a plant

atmosphere   the layer of air around the Earth

atom   the smallest unit of an element that still behaves like the element

bedrock   a layer of solid rock below the subsoil

carbon dioxide   a gas made up of carbon and oxygen atoms

chlorophyll   a substance in plants that enables them to absorb light from the Sun and use this energy to make food

climate   the average weather conditions in an area over a long period of time

cold-blooded   having a body temperature that changes and adapts to the temperature of the environment

condensation   the formation of a liquid from a gas by cooling

conduction   transferring heat or electricity or other forms of energy from one place to another

crust   the rocky, outer layer of Earth's surface

density   the weight of an object or substance compared to the amount of space it occupies

eclipse   the casting of a shadow across a body in space by the passing of another body in space

electron   a very tiny particle of matter that contains a negative charge and usually orbits around the center of an atom

energy   the ability to do work

environment   the surroundings in which plants and animals live

evaporation   the changing of a liquid to a gas through heat or the motion of air

expand   to become larger

fossil   the remains of ancient living things

friction	the resistance to movement between one object and another as their surfaces pass each other
groundwater	water beneath Earth's surface
lubricant	a substance used to reduce friction
machine	a device used to do work
mass	the amount of matter in a substance
matter	the substance of which everything in the universe is made
metamorphosis	the development of certain animals in four stages from egg to adult
molecule	the smallest particle of a substance that can exist alone and has all the characteristics of that substance—molecules are made up of atoms
nucleus	the center of an atom, containing protons and neutrons
orbit	the path of an object in space around another object
photosynthesis	the process green plants use to convert water, sunlight, and carbon dioxide to food
plant	a living thing that is not an animal
precipitation	the condensation of water vapor from the atmosphere—rain, snow, and fog are forms of precipitation
propulsion	a force that pushes an object forward
reproduction	the process by which a living thing produces another organism like itself
solution	one or more substances dissolved in another, usually liquid, substances
spore	the reproductive cell of certain living things
surface tension	the force produced by the thin film at the surface of a liquid
topsoil	the uppermost fertile layer of soil on Earth's crust
vapor	a substance that is in a gaseous form
vibration	a rapid movement back and forth or up and down
volume	the amount of space an object or substance occupies
warm-blooded	having a body temperature that is unchanged by the temperature of the environment

Index